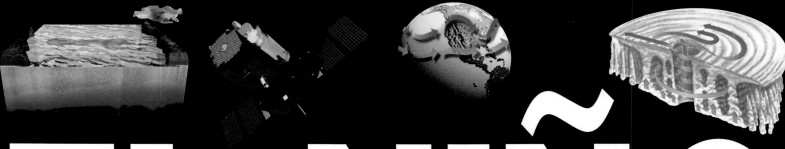

THE NEW BOOK OF

EL NIÑO

Simon Beecroft

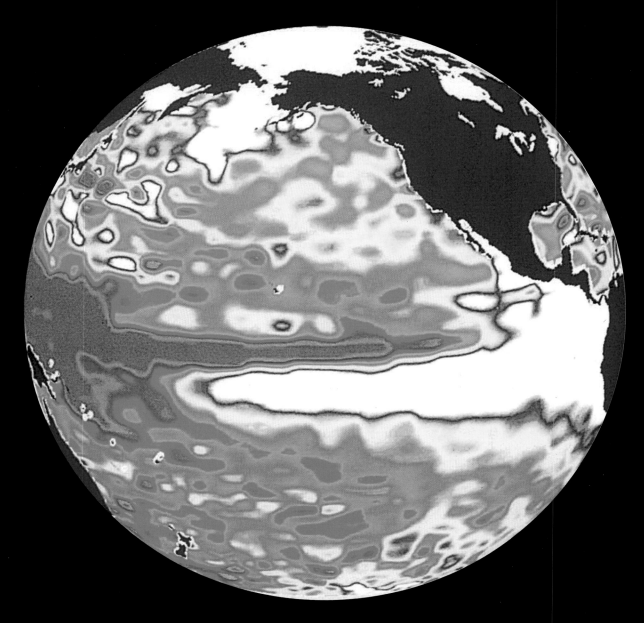

COPPER BEECH BOOKS
BROOKFIELD, CONNECTICUT

Contents

© Aladdin Books Ltd 1999
Designed and produced by
Aladdin Books Ltd
28 Percy Street
London W1P 0LD

*First published in the
United States in 1999 by*
Copper Beech Books,
an imprint of
The Millbrook Press
2 Old New Milford Road
Brookfield, Connecticut 06804

Printed in Belgium
All rights reserved

Editor
Jim Pipe
Design
David West
Children's Book Design
Designer
Flick Killerby
Illustrators
Richard Rockwood
& Rob Shone
Picture Research
Brooks Krikler Research

Library of Congress Cataloging-in-Publication Data
Beecroft, Simon.
The new book of El Niño / by Simon Beecroft.
p. cm.
Summary: Describes the causes and effects of the unusual weather
phenomenon known as El Niño.
ISBN 0-7613-0920-9 (lib. bdg.). — ISBN 0-7613-0797-4 (pbk.)
1. El Niño Current—Juvenile literature. [1. El Niño Current.]
I. Title.
GC296.8.E4B44 1999   98-55560
551.5'24642—dc21   CIP AC

5 4 3 2 1

INTRODUCTION

The 1997-1998 El Niño (*el neen-yo*) brought disaster to the world. It created droughts, hurricanes, and forest fires, and helped the spread of deadly diseases. Millions of people were affected by it across the world.

El Niño is the movement of warm water in the eastern Pacific Ocean that happens every three to seven years. However, the earth's delicate weather system means it can affect events on the other side of the planet.

This mysterious phenomenon has been around for several thousand years. But in the last 15 years, El Niños seem to have caused much more violent weather. As a result, El Niño is now the focus of several major projects to predict the weather, not days, but months ahead.

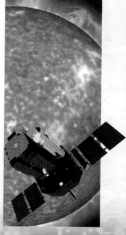

The disastrous 1982-1983 and 1997-1998 El Niños made many scientists realize that they needed to be able to predict the weather months in advance. To help them, they are investigating other events that dramatically affect the weather, such as solar activity and volcanic eruptions.

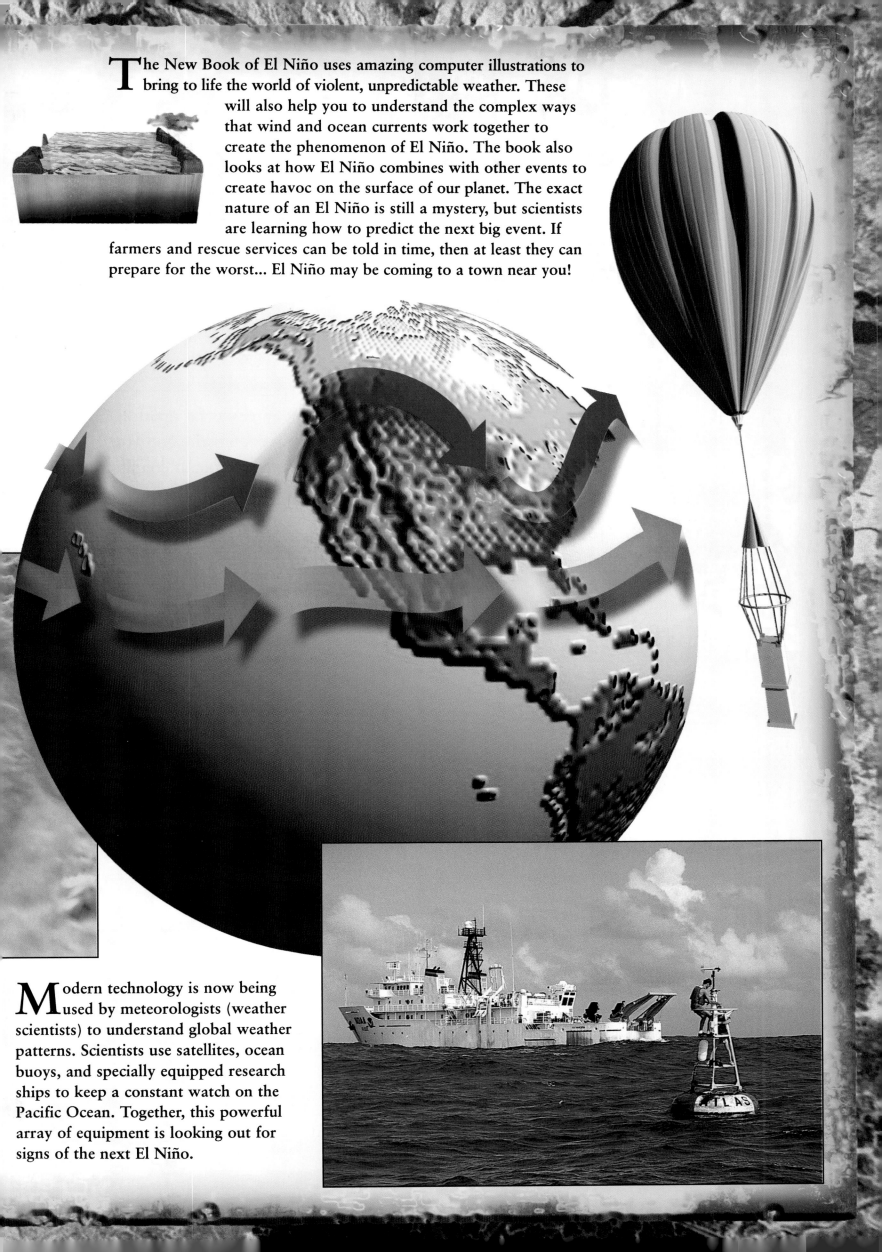

The New Book of El Niño uses amazing computer illustrations to bring to life the world of violent, unpredictable weather. These will also help you to understand the complex ways that wind and ocean currents work together to create the phenomenon of El Niño. The book also looks at how El Niño combines with other events to create havoc on the surface of our planet. The exact nature of an El Niño is still a mystery, but scientists are learning how to predict the next big event. If farmers and rescue services can be told in time, then at least they can prepare for the worst... El Niño may be coming to a town near you!

Modern technology is now being used by meteorologists (weather scientists) to understand global weather patterns. Scientists use satellites, ocean buoys, and specially equipped research ships to keep a constant watch on the Pacific Ocean. Together, this powerful array of equipment is looking out for signs of the next El Niño.

CHAPTER ONE

THE BRINGER OF STORMS

Weather is always strange. No year goes by without a hottest day or a wettest month in some part of the world. But in some years, the world experiences a run of freak weather — sudden, unexpected storms, long periods of drought, torrential mudslides, and nightmare blizzards. Few areas escape some kind of natural disaster.

And what is often the cause for all this? El Niño. This is not a new phenomenon. It has upset weather patterns for centuries. But for some reason, in the last 15 years two particularly strong El Niños brought chaos to the world. They affected nearly every area of life, including farming, transportation, health, even the food that was available on the other side of the planet. As a result, scientists are now battling to uncover the mysteries of El Niño.

DRYING UP THE RAINS

During the 1982 El Niño, areas as far apart as California, England, Australia, Indonesia, Siberia, and South Africa experienced some of the worst drought conditions this century. In South Africa, 80 percent of its commercial corn crop was lost, while the drought in southeast England was the worst since the 18th century.

In Indonesia, El Niño brings unusually hot, dry weather. Forests become dry and catch fire easily. In November 1997 an area of forest the size of California and Nevada was affected by fire. Smoke from the burning forests was blamed for airplane and shipping accidents that killed 300 people.

EL NIÑO FLOODING

Somalia in East Africa is a hot, dry country with little rainfall. But in 1997-1998, El Niño brought sudden, unexpected rainstorms to the area (*above*). Instead of the usual drought conditions, Somalians had to deal with flooded villages and waterlogged fields, producing the worst harvest in 130 years.

CAUSING A SPIN

El Niño's effect on wind patterns may cause the earth to rotate more slowly, creating fractionally longer days. This striking example of El Niño's power was detected using an array of over 100 radio telescopes across the globe. But this doesn't mean you can spend longer in bed — scientists calculated that our day is now 0.4 milliseconds longer!

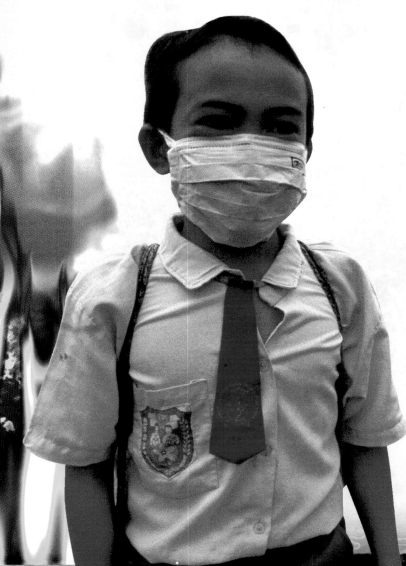

During dry weather periods set off by El Niño, raging forest fires produce smog. This causes an increase in breathing problems in humans. In 1997, Indonesian aid workers handed out face masks to thousands of people to combat the harmful effects of smog (*left*). But because an El Niño does not happen every year, scientists will have to wait to uncover its true long-term effects.

WHAT IS EL NIÑO?

El Niño means "the Christ Child" in Spanish. It was first named in the 17th century by Spanish-speaking fishermen. They lived in Peru, a country on the west coast of South America. They noticed that the cold waters off Peru became warmer each year around Christmas, the traditional time of Christ's birth. Then, every few years, this warming effect was stronger than usual.

In the 1970s, scientists saw that big El Niños influenced the world's weather. They knew that the oceans and atmosphere work together to control the earth's temperature. The oceans on the equator soak up heat from the sun. Then the earth's spin mixes this heat with cold air from the poles. This stops the oceans from getting too hot, and the poles from getting too cold. When El Niño occurs, this balance is disturbed — with powerful results.

The Atacama Desert in Peru (below) is brought to life by El Niño.

Storm clouds

← Trade winds blow warm surface waters to west.

PACIFIC OCEAN

AUSTRALIA

Warm water in west creates storm clouds. ← Strong currents hold warm water in place. Cold water rises from deep.

El Niño occurs off the Pacific coast of South America.

IN A NORMAL YEAR

More of the sun's rays hit the Pacific than any other ocean. This makes the seas here very warm. In a normal year, winds push the warmed surface waters to the west where they are held in place by ocean currents (*top*). This leaves a deep pool of very warm water off the coast of Australia. The warm waters evaporate quickly, creating storm clouds over Australia in December. Off the coast of South America, the warm waters are replaced by cold waters rising from the ocean depths. They leave Peru and Ecuador without rain.

March 1997: The white/red patch *May 1997: As El Niño begins, the*

**NORMAL
YEAR**

SOUTH
AMERICA

THE BABY GIRL

El Niño does not always mean disaster. For example, the Atacama Desert in Peru is usually a dry, barren scrubland (*page 6*). When El Niño strikes, it rains heavily on the desert, causing it to bloom with a carpet of flowers.

In some years, La Niña ("the Little Girl") occurs when there is no El Niño. La Niñas make the waters near Peru become even colder, with the opposite effects to El Niño. Elsewhere, areas that are warmer during El Niño instead become cold and wet; areas that are colder become warmer. For example, in Indonesia and Australia, La Niña brings rain and good conditions for farming (*right*).

*Weak winds fail to keep
warm water in the west.*

*Storm clouds
over South
America*

**EL NIÑO
YEAR**

AUSTRALIA

PACIFIC OCEAN

SOUTH
AMERICA

*Water in west
cooler than usual*

*Strong current helps to
push warm water east.* →

*Warm water
in the east*

Cold water trapped on bottom by layer of warm water

*October 1997: El Niño continues
to heat up the Pacific waters.*

WHAT HAPPENS IN AN EL NIÑO YEAR?

In a big El Niño year, the winds and currents that hold the warm water near Australia weaken or reverse. So the warm water moves east toward the coast of South America (*above*). Here it creates the rain clouds that normally fall over Australia. Meanwhile, the unusually cool waters near Australia fail to produce rain, causing drought. Satellite photographs show the warm water as a huge white/red gash across the Pacific (*left*).

CHAPTER TWO

EL NIÑO *WORLDWIDE*

If El Niño affected just the Pacific Ocean, it would not be headline news. But the warming of the Pacific waters off the coast of South America produces unpredictable and violent weather across the globe.

In El Niño years, the unusually warm waters off the coast of South America create thunderstorms. These pump warm, humid air more than 5,000 feet (1,500 meters) into the sky. This warm air changes the course of high-altitude winds, called jet stream winds. For example, the jet stream storms that are usually carried north toward Alaska are pushed eastward and end up flooding southern California. The jet streams head west to continents as far away as Africa and Europe. The effects of El Niño on these distant regions are very difficult to predict. Some areas may experience flooding in one El Niño year, then drought the next.

IN THE JET STREAM

The jet streams that affect the routes of airplaines and high-altitude balloons (*below*) are sent off course by El Niño. Flying with these high-speed winds increases speed and saves on fuel. Then pilots avoid the winds when they are flying back in the opposite direction, so they are not slowed down.

This effect was first noticed during World War II when U.S. bombers heading westward found they flew very slowly. Yet, when they turned back, they found they were helped along by winds of over 180 mph (300 km/h).

The map below shows the areas affected by storms and drought during the 1991 El Niño. Some of the worst hit regions were:
1. U.S.A. — Hurricane Bob caused $1.8 billion of damage.
2. Peru — suffered worst drought this century.
3. Malawi — 50,000 lost their homes to mudslides.
4. Ethiopia — 7 million affected by drought.
5. China — floods killed 2,295 and injured 50,000.
6. Indonesia — massive forest fires in Borneo.
7. Australia — worst harvest in 20 years.

KEY

Drought

Severe storms

The two most important jet stream winds are the subtropical jet and the polar jet (*right*). In the El Niño of late 1991, the subtropical jet stream brought unusually heavy rain to the Gulf of Mexico. The polar jet stream pumped warm air far toward the Arctic Circle. That year winter temperatures in Canada were several degrees above normal.

There is no such thing as a normal El Niño. During most El Niño years, winters in the northern United States and Canada are warmer than usual. Storms (*below*) rage in normally dry areas of Peru, Ecuador, and the eastern United States, while Australia, Indonesia, and the Philippines are hit by drought. But in other El Niño years, these dry areas are flooded, and Peru is hit by drought — that's the mystery of El Niño.

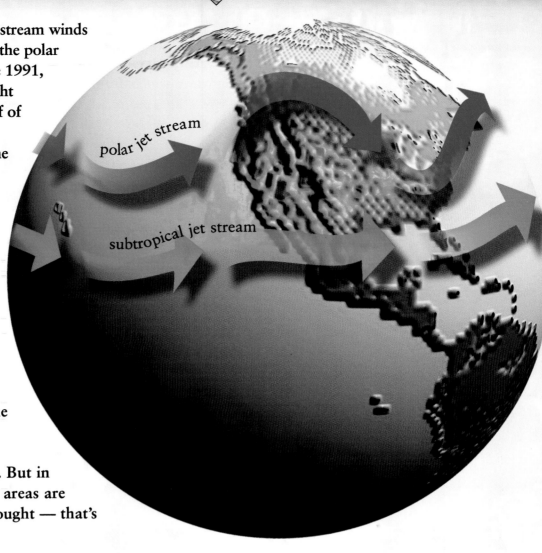

polar jet stream

subtropical jet stream

WHAT ARE JET STREAM WINDS?

Jet streams are fast-moving ribbons of wind that travel for thousands of miles from east to west. They are an important part of the weather system that mixes warm air from the equator with cold air from the poles. Jet streams reach speeds of up to about 280 mph (500 km/h) and move at altitudes of 25,000 – 40,000 feet (7,500 – 12,000 m).

DEALING WITH DISASTER

When El Niño strikes, rescue teams around the world are put on emergency standby (*below*). Flash floods and tidal waves destroy homes and roads, killing thousands of people and leaving millions homeless. The 1997-1998 El Niño alone caused damage costing billions of dollars. Flooding also destroys crops and causes mudslides and landslides. Drought can easily destroy a harvest, leading to widespread famine.

Floods caused by El Niño can also help the spread of deadly diseases such as malaria, cholera, typhoid, and yellow fever.

ENDANGERED WILDLIFE

El Niño can have a dramatic effect on animals around the world. When El Niño brings warm water to the eastern Pacific Ocean, cold-water fish are driven away. This is disastrous for the Peruvian fishing industry. Seabirds such as pelicans, cormorants, and boobies need these fish to survive, and many sea lions also die if the fish disappear.

In the 1950s, about 28 million sea birds lived off the coast of Peru. By 1982-1983, when there was a severe El Niño, the number had dropped to about 2 million. Meanwhile, starving pelicans and sea lions were killing their own kind to survive.

Seals and sea lions are also affected in California. In El Niño years, the salmon they usually feed on swim farther north to waters off Canada. Farther south, in Antarctica, fewer seals are born every time there is an El Niño year.

Marine iguanas can only be found in the Galápagos Islands in the eastern Pacific Ocean. But the lizards are being threatened by the warm waters that El Niño brings. They feed on cold-water seaweeds. But as the waters around the islands warm up, these seaweeds die out. They are replaced by warm-water-loving seaweeds that the lizards cannot eat.

Shoals of small fish, particularly anchovies, live in the Pacific Ocean near Peru. They feed on the tiny plants and animals that live in colder waters. In a normal year, currents drag this cold water up from the deep. But in an El Niño year, the currents bring warm waters from the west. This reduces the number of tiny plants and creatures in the sea. The anchovies then swim south to colder water or starve from lack of food. This is causing problems for Peru's fishermen (*right*).

El Niño also affects the Peruvian guano industry. Guano is the nutrient-packed droppings of seabirds. It is collected from local rocks (*above left*) and used as fertilizer. Usually, thousands of seabirds create big mounds of guano. But when El Niño strikes, the warm waters drive the anchovies away. This leaves the seabirds without their main food supply (*below right*). Either the seabirds die out, or they follow the fish to colder waters farther south.

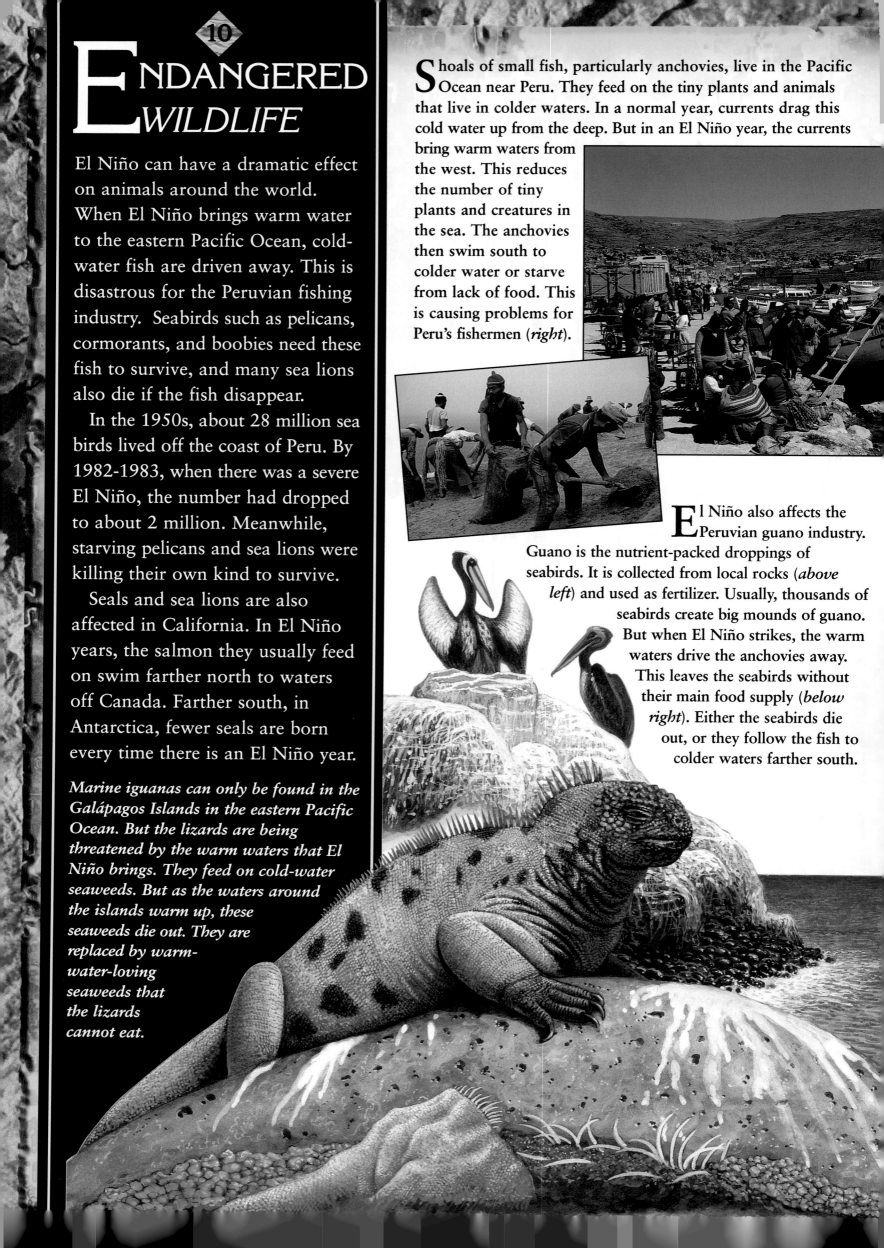

RAINFOREST WILDLIFE

Rainforest animals are threatened by El Niño's bizarre weather. In places like Indonesia, where El Niño causes drought, forests easily catch fire. Animals such as orangutans (*below*) flee to the edges of the forest to escape the flames. Here they become easy targets for predators, including human poachers. On the nearby island of Borneo, rare animals, such as howler monkeys (*right*), face extinction if rain does not fall regularly.

CORAL REEFS

El Niño is putting coral reefs in danger (*right*). Coral reefs are made of the hard skeletons of millions of coral animals. The coral animals get food from algae that live in their bodies. But when the sea warms up during an El Niño event, the algae leave the coral. Without the algae the coral animals die.

WILDLIFE SURVIVORS

El Niño is not always harmful to wildlife. In some areas that are usually dry for long periods, it brings much-needed rain. This provides water and food for the animals that live there.

Even the hot, dry weather El Niño creates can help wildlife. In the Panamanian rainforest in Central America, El Niño brings sunshine to usually cloudy areas. This helps seeds and fruit to grow, providing more food for rainforest animals.

In Somalia in Africa, heavy rains ended a period of terrible drought. The animals there (*below*) took advantage of the extra food and water created by the rains. But for human beings the flooding was devastating. However, just as farmers take advantage of the changing seasons, so the better we predict El Niño, the more we may even be able to take advantage of the unusual weather it brings.

Giant tortoises, which live only on the remote Galápagos Islands, have learned to take advantage of El Niño. Scientists have noticed that the annual growth rings in the tortoises' shells reveal growth spurts in El Niño years. This is because El Niño brings unusually long and heavy rainfall, which produces bumper crops of the vegetation that the tortoises feed on.

SAVING THE HIPPOS

In 1992 in South Africa, El Niño brought a long drought. Among the casualties of this dry weather were hippopotamuses. Many hundreds of these rare wild animals died, and the species as a whole was threatened.

However, some farmers, realizing the threat, took action. They built enclosures to protect the hippos. The farmers made sure these endangered animals were fed, even at the cost of their own sheep and cattle (*main picture*). In a few years, their life-saving work paid off, as hippos began to fill the rivers and watering holes again.

A SPEEDY RECOVERY

Kelp is a kind of seaweed that grows into giant floating columns, like underwater forests (*right*). A single column can measure up to 200 feet (60 m) long. Sea kelp provides shelter for fish and lobsters and food for many marine animals, such as snails and sea urchins. In 1992 El Niño warmed the waters off the coast of California, which uprooted the giant sea kelp that lived there. However, the damage was not permanent. In less than a year these towering stacks recovered and grew back.

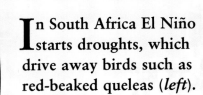

In South Africa El Niño starts droughts, which drive away birds such as red-beaked queleas (*left*). However, as the effects grow weaker, the land has time to recover. Grass grows again and acts as a sponge, drawing up water from underground so that trees grow tall and strong again. These trees provide homes for birds and other wildlife, which begin to return in large numbers.

CHAPTER THREE

WHY BLAME EL NIÑO?

El Niño is a warning to us of how delicately balanced the weather is on Earth, and how easily massive changes can occur. Scientists are now looking at the links between the recent big El Niños and other changes in the world's weather.

One change is global warming. This is the gradual overheating of the earth due to the buildup of heat-trapping gases in the atmosphere. On its own, global warming could create other serious problems, such as huge forest fires (*below*) and severe flooding if the ice caps melt.

An enormous amount of research is being done, using sophisticated equipment, such as satellites and weather balloons. Even using these, El Niño remains a mystery. It is not always clear whether higher temperatures should be blamed on El Niño, on global warming, or on a mix of the two.

WEATHER NET

Scientists use computers to make complex models of weather conditions (*below*). A new state-of-the-art computer network, called Advanced Weather Interactive Processing System (AWIPS), is now being tested. It will allow scientists all over the world to examine more closely regions hit by violent weather.

Weather balloon

WATER VAPOR

Water vapor (water as a gas) is one of the main gases that trap sunlight in the atmosphere and add to the warming effect of the planet. Water goes around in a continuous cycle. It evaporates (changes from a liquid into a gas) as it rises from oceans, lakes, and rivers. Up in the atmosphere, it forms clouds. Then the water returns to the earth as rain and snow. But as increasingly severe El Niños warm up the Pacific Ocean, more water evaporates. This makes the atmosphere even warmer. However, since extra cloud cover also shades the earth's surface from the sun's rays, scientists are not certain which effect is the stronger.

Rainfall

Evaporation

WEATHER SATELLITES

Weather satellites (*above*) are a useful source of data on global warming. One of the latest projects is NASA's TIROS-N satellites. These measure the temperature of layers in the atmosphere. Until the 1980s, readings were taken using surface-based computer models. According to these, the planet seemed to be warmer than ever before. But the findings of TIROS-N suggest that Earth is actually growing colder.

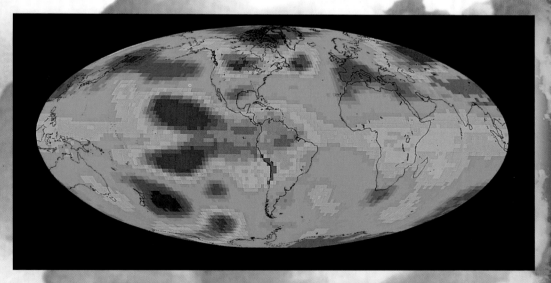

The TIROS-N satellite produced this image of the strong 1982-1983 El Niño. The red areas indicate higher-than-average temperatures, while the blue areas are lower-than-average temperatures.

The latest remote-operated weather balloons take readings as they rise higher and higher into the atmosphere (*left*). They measure temperature, humidity, and pressure, as well as wind speed, and send this information back to the ground using instruments called radiosondes.

VOLCANOES & EARTHQUAKES

Another reason El Niño is so mysterious is that volcanoes and earthquakes can confuse researchers. Volcanoes, too, create warm sea currents and can also cover up the effects of El Niños by filling the atmosphere with gas and ash.

The largest volcanic eruptions shoot clouds of gas, ash, and dust high into the air. These clouds drift around the world and block out sunlight for months, or even years. Some scientists believe that the warm currents of El Niño may even be started by underwater volcanoes (*below*).

Scientists have studied several recent eruptions using the new wave of sophisticated technology. They were able to monitor the effects of these eruptions using high-tech satellite images and remote-sensing instruments.

MOUNT PINATUBO ERUPTS

In 1991 Mount Pinatubo, a volcano in the Philippines, erupted after a 600-year silence (*below*). The event was tracked from space by NASA's Earth Radiation Budget Experiment. A dust cloud made up of 25-30 million tons of material was shot up into the air and circled the globe in just three weeks. Two months later, almost half the earth's surface was covered up by dust, cooling the planet by 0.9°F (0.5°C) in that year.

When the Mexican volcano El Chichón erupted in 1982, a cloud of gases was blasted out. The cloud blocked the vision of satellites watching out for El Niño events. The effect was to make sea surface temperatures appear cooler, which hid the warm waters of El Niño that year.

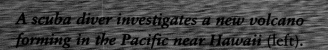

A scuba diver investigates a new volcano forming in the Pacific near Hawaii (left).

STUDYING VOLCANOES

In 1983, the Total Ozone Mapping Spectrometer (TOMS) project was launched. This measures sulfur dioxide levels in eruption clouds (*below*). Scientists now understand that sulfur dioxide, given out by erupting volcanoes, is much more effective than ash or dust at reflecting the sun's heat back into space. This lowers world temperatures and covers up the warming effects of an El Niño.

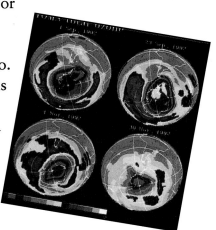

Another project to track volcanic eruptions is NASA's Earth Observing System (EOS). Launched in 1998, this system consists of a series of satellites that orbit the north and south poles. The satellites' sensors determine the height of an eruption cloud and can produce realistic 3-D models of it.

June 16, 1991

June 20, 1991

June 24, 1991

June 28, 1991

Today, scientists are using satellites to track the clouds formed by volcanic eruptions while the clouds are spreading. For example, they followed the clouds created by Mount Pinatubo in 1991 as they drifted across southern Asia and Africa (*above*).

Satellites do this using remote sensors that detect radiation and other invisible forms of energy given off by the volcano. They also study what is in the clouds. The more ash and sulfur dioxide there is, the lower the temperature of the air and sea below.

The eruption of El Chichón in 1982 covered some of the Mayan pyramids of Palenque with ash. There was so much ash it settled like snow on these huge stone structures (*above*).

ICE AGES IN *THE FUTURE*

The strange mix of El Niños and La Niñas makes it even harder to predict the future. In the last 20 years, seven El Niños have occurred, and only three La Niñas. This has resulted in an overall warming trend. But a string of strong La Niñas would lower temperatures. El Niño also has a companion in the Atlantic Ocean, called the North Atlantic Oscillation (NAO), which has warm and cold phases like El Niño and La Niña.

At one extreme, an ice age could be triggered, when ice covers large regions of land. Several ice ages have taken place in the earth's history, each lasting a few million years. The last began about two million years ago and ended about 10,000 years ago. Ice ages are usually caused by a change in the relative distance of the earth from the sun (*see page 19*). But could a run of extreme La Niñas or El Niños create an icy future?

POLAR PATROL

When an ice age begins, huge sheets of ice, called glaciers (*below*), spread south from the north pole. In the last ice age much of northern Europe, Asia, and North America were completely covered by ice. Now, earth scientists based in the Arctic, the area around the north pole, are closely watching glaciers to see if they are moving south.

As a result of the severe El Niño event in 1991, New York was hit by the worst ice storm it had seen for decades. The raging blizzard knocked out power to more than 300,000 homes. A string of El Niños following each other closely could cause freezing on a massive scale (*main picture*).

THE LITTLE ICE AGE

Between about 1600 and 1800, Great Britain and North America experienced a period of unusually cold weather known as the Little Ice Age (*below left* and *right*). The Thames River in London and the Hudson River in New York regularly froze over, and "frost fairs" were held on the ice. More seriously, the population of Iceland, farther north, was nearly wiped out by the freeze. Weather scientists think this period of bizarre weather may have been set off by a strong El Niño.

IRREGULAR ORBIT

An important influence on ice ages is the change in the earth's orbit around the sun (*below*). The orbit can grow larger over periods of 100,000 years.

The distance between the earth and the sun can differ by as much as 11 million miles (18 million km), enough to cause massive heat and climatic changes on Earth.

SPACE WEATHER

Energy from the the sun drives all weather on Earth. But changes on the sun's surface can also trigger violent changes in our planet's outer atmosphere. Some of these may affect the strength of El Niños.

Space weather, a new field of science, aims to predict the effects of weather from space on the earth. About 50 years ago, most scientists believed that the earth was surrounded by empty, unchanging space. The launch of the first satellites in the 1950s changed all that. Now we know that space is filled with activity — much of it caused by the sun.

A major part of the global effort to understand our star and its effects on our environment is the Solar and Heliospheric Observatory (SOHO) spacecraft. Run by NASA and the European Space Agency, SOHO observes the sun from a point 0.6 million miles (one million km) in front of the earth.

The sun produces a hot gas, called solar wind, that travels through space at about one million mph (1.6 million km/h). The earth is protected from this powerful solar wind by an enormous force field called the magnetosphere (*below*). However, some solar wind energy does enter the magnetosphere and can disrupt our atmosphere. Scientists do not yet know how this might affect the earth's climate in the long term.

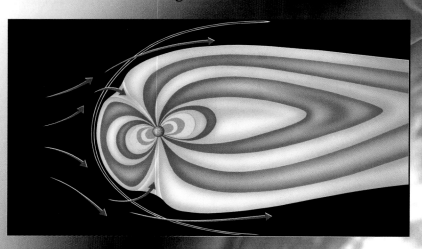

The magneto (above) pro earth from high-ener particles created by solar flares.

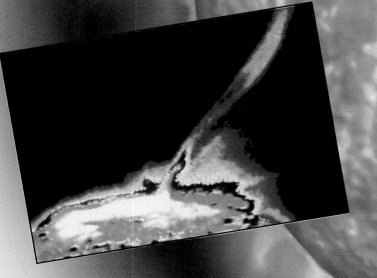

The sun is thought to go through periods of increased solar activity, characterized by sunspots and solar flares (*above*). Scientists have found evidence, such as the growth rings of trees (*left*), that show long periods of warming and cooling. Solar activity may affect this warming of the planet and may even be responsible for some of the events blamed on El Niño.

WATCHING THE SUN

As well as creating solar wind, the sun's radiation causes air currents and makes clouds and rain. But studying this weather-maker through an ordinary telescope would make you blind. Instead, special instruments, such as radio telescopes, are used to detect the sun's radiation (*below*). Telescopes in space are also used to study the sun's X rays and gamma rays, since these weaker emissions cannot get through the Earth's atmosphere.

The SOHO spacecraft (*below*) allows scientists a "ringside seat" from which to study the sun. It gives them the first warning of solar activity that may affect satellites and equipment on Earth.

OUT OF ORBIT

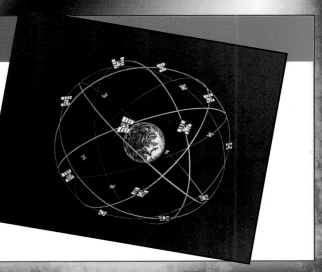

When the particles from a solar flare hit the earth's magnetic field, they can knock satellites (*right*) and spacecraft out of orbit. They also cause television static on Earth and create power blackouts. In addition, they produce navigation problems for ships and airplanes with magnetic compasses. Solar flares may have little effect on the weather in our atmosphere. But given the massive force of a solar flare (10 million times the power of a volcanic explosion), scientists are now trying to find out what this impact might be.

CHAPTER FOUR
OCEAN STUDIES

The destruction created by recent El Niños has forced scientists to look more closely at how the oceans influence the weather. We have already seen how ocean currents, along with winds, help to keep the earth at a steady temperature by moving heat from the equator to the polar regions. Warm and cold currents also influence temperatures on land, like the Gulf Stream that warms the British Isles.

Meteorologists are also learning to look much farther ahead. Thanks to a new system of sensors, they knew the strong 1997-1998 El Niño was coming months in advance. Projects such as TOGA/TAO (*page 24*) and WOCE (*page 23*) are studying the effects of the ocean on weather. Once El Niño can be accurately predicted, we can prepare for it just as we get ready for winter or spring.

SUBMERSIBLES

Submersibles (*left*) are a type of submarine that take scientists down deep into the ocean to carry out studies. A recent project, called Operation Vivaldi, studied the workings of the polar sink in the far North Atlantic (*see below*). Robot submersibles were used to make regular journeys beneath the ice to see how much of it was melting due to global warming.

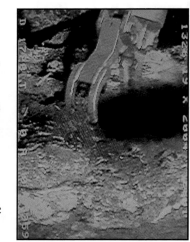

Exploring the ocean floor is one way of finding out about the changing climate (*right*). The ocean floor is made up of layers of dead organisms that were laid down over centuries. Drilling through the layers of the ocean floor reveals different types and numbers of organisms. These tell scientists what the climate was like in a particular period.

POLAR SINK

The "polar sink" is part of the ocean "conveyor belt" that carries energy from the sun. Surface currents such as the Gulf Stream carry heat from tropical regions toward the polar regions. There the water loses heat to the atmosphere. The "sink" occurs because freezing seawater squeezes out salt. This makes the water heavier, so it sinks. Deep currents carry this cold water back to the tropics. If the polar sink stopped, the result would make countries like Great Britain and France more like Alaska.

2. Heat is lost to air.

3. Freezing seawater squeezes out salt, so water sinks down.

1. Warm currents arrive from the tropics.

4. Cold, deep water is carried back to equator.

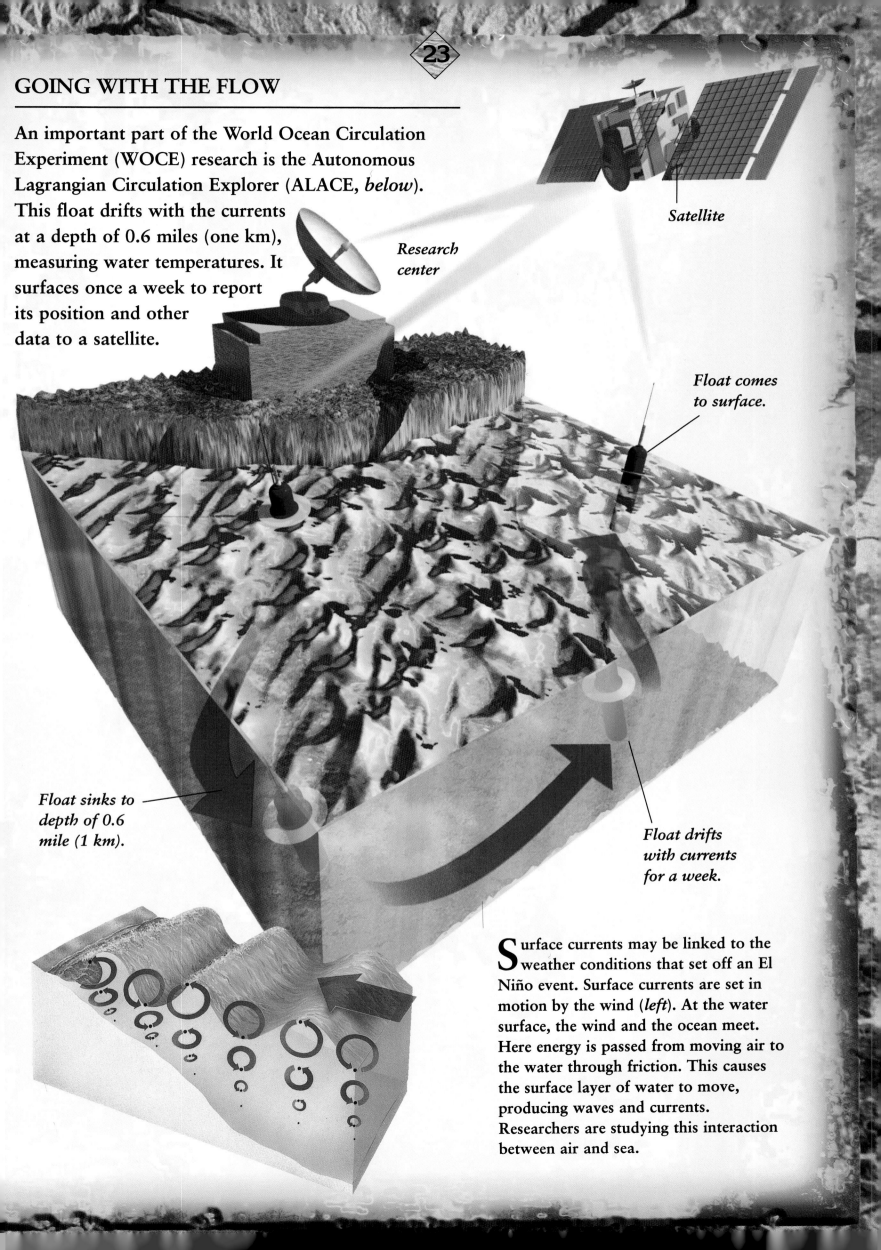

GOING WITH THE FLOW

An important part of the World Ocean Circulation Experiment (WOCE) research is the Autonomous Lagrangian Circulation Explorer (ALACE, *below*). This float drifts with the currents at a depth of 0.6 miles (one km), measuring water temperatures. It surfaces once a week to report its position and other data to a satellite.

Research center

Satellite

Float comes to surface.

Float sinks to depth of 0.6 mile (1 km).

Float drifts with currents for a week.

Surface currents may be linked to the weather conditions that set off an El Niño event. Surface currents are set in motion by the wind (*left*). At the water surface, the wind and the ocean meet. Here energy is passed from moving air to the water through friction. This causes the surface layer of water to move, producing waves and currents. Researchers are studying this interaction between air and sea.

TRACKING & PREDICTING

In 1997, the most sophisticated weather-forecasting computer predicted that the Pacific Ocean would be cold for the rest of the year — the opposite of an El Niño. But, by the end of that year, the fastest-occurring and strongest El Niño ever recorded was surging across the ocean to wreak havoc in the east. Researchers were forced to accept that computers could not predict El Niño using historical data.

Luckily, scientists have found more practical ways of looking for early signs of El Niño. After the 1982-1983 event, the Tropical Ocean Global Atmosphere/Tropical Atmosphere Ocean array (TOGA/ TAO) was set up. This system provides almost instant information using a satellite link. Its data comes from a grid of moored ATLAS (*see page 25*) buoys, drifters, and tide gauges.

A GRID ACROSS THE PACIFIC

The TOGA/TAO project uses instruments that stretch for thousands of miles across the Pacific Ocean. Approximately 70 ATLAS buoys track changes in the ocean and air and relay this information via satellite (*below*). The TOGA system also uses drifters, which follow ocean currents. Tide gauges placed on Pacific islands monitor changing sea levels (one sign of an El Niño). The system puts together the information from this grid of sensors to create a complete picture covering the Pacific.

Since El Niño events only occur every few years, there are not enough data to make reliable predictions using just experience.

But the TOGA/TAO project is in constant operation in the tropical Pacific Ocean, watching changes in temperature, winds, and storms (*left*). It gives scientists up-to-date information to feed into their computer models and may give the first warning that an El Niño event is developing.

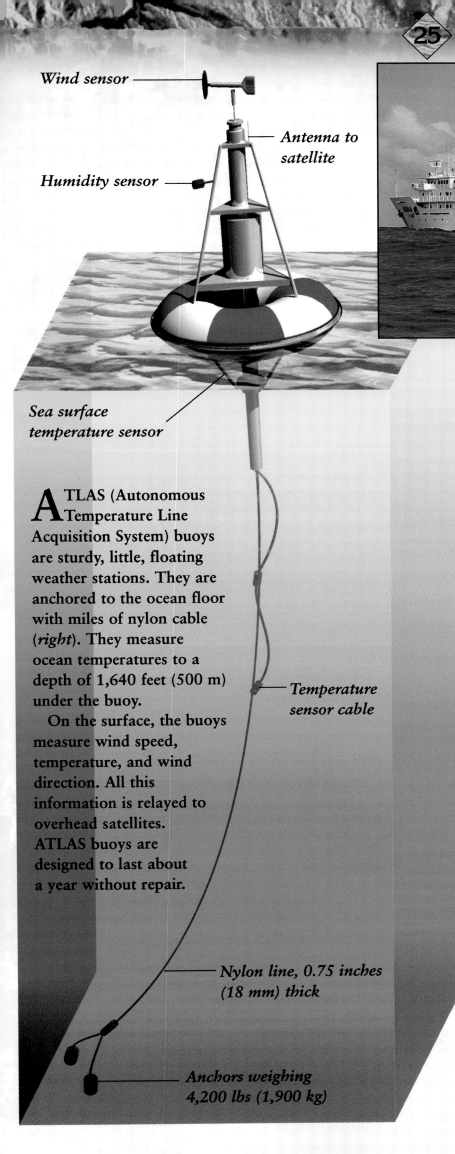

Wind sensor

Antenna to
satellite

Humidity sensor

Sea surface
temperature sensor

ATLAS (Autonomous
Temperature Line
Acquisition System) buoys
are sturdy, little, floating
weather stations. They are
anchored to the ocean floor
with miles of nylon cable
(*right*). They measure
ocean temperatures to a
depth of 1,640 feet (500 m)
under the buoy.
  On the surface, the buoys
measure wind speed,
temperature, and wind
direction. All this
information is relayed to
overhead satellites.
ATLAS buoys are
designed to last about
a year without repair.

Temperature
sensor cable

Nylon line, 0.75 inches
(18 mm) thick

Anchors weighing
4,200 lbs (1,900 kg)

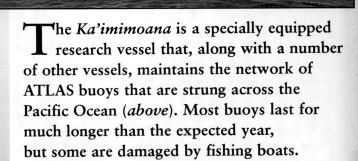

The *Ka'imimoana* is a specially equipped
research vessel that, along with a number
of other vessels, maintains the network of
ATLAS buoys that are strung across the
Pacific Ocean (*above*). Most buoys last for
much longer than the expected year,
but some are damaged by fishing boats.

TESTING THE OCEANS

XBTs (Expendable Bathythermographs)
measure temperature and pressure in the
top layer of the ocean. They are thrown
off the sides of ships that are traveling at
full speed. Chemicals in the water are
measured by a water-sampling rosette
(*below*). As it is lowered, its bottles are
filled at different depths. Salt in the water
is checked by a CTD (Conductivity-
Temperature-Density) instrument.

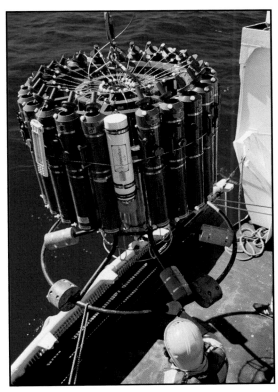

TROPICAL STORMS

Scientists are also measuring the tropical storms created by El Niño. These storms are called hurricanes, cyclones, or typhoons, depending on where they occur. They are high-speed, spinning winds that carry heavy rains. They form during late summer near the tropics and move westward, causing phenomenal destruction to places they hit.

When the Pacific Ocean is warmer than usual because of El Niño, fewer hurricanes develop in the Atlantic Ocean, but more cyclones and typhoons are whipped up in the Pacific. El Niño's opposite, La Niña, cools the tropical waters and makes it more likely for Atlantic hurricanes to develop. In 1998, La Niña created the deadliest hurricane season for two centuries. In total, 14 hurricanes occurred, including the devastating Hurricane Mitch, which claimed the lives of at least 10,000 people.

Hurricane Fran, which devastated North Carolina in September 1996, was the third-most costly hurricane in U.S. history (*above*).

CAMEX-3

CAMEX-3, begun in 1998, is the first project since the 1950s to study the highly destructive upper levels of a hurricane (usually, the less dangerous middle levels are investigated). CAMEX-3 uses modified DC-8s and ER-2s, the research version of the U-2 spy plane (*above right*). These aircraft are equipped with high-tech instruments that record and measure lightning, water vapor content, and rainfall. The planes are also equipped with lasers that measure wind speed by scanning dust and droplets carried in the wind.

The winds on the edge of a hurricane can reach speeds of 133 mph (240 km/h, *left*). The chance of two or more hurricanes hitting the United States during a La Niña year is more than double that of an El Niño year.

INTO THE STORM

On a typical CAMEX-3 mission, the ER-2 and a DC-8 fly in parallel above the hurricane. They cross it several times in a figure of eight pattern (*right*). At a number of points the aircraft parachute instrument packages into the storm (*main picture*). On one of the crosses, the DC-8 spirals down into the eye (the center) of the storm to carry out detailed measurements. The data are then put on the internet for use by researchers worldwide.

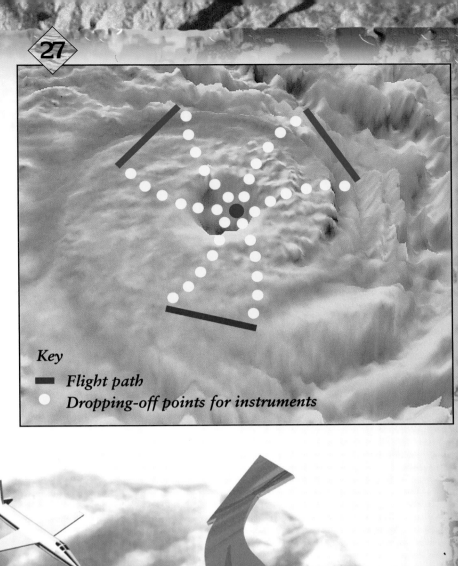

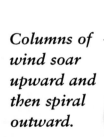

Key

━━━ *Flight path*

○ *Dropping-off points for instruments*

Columns of wind soar upward and then spiral outward.

Swirling bands of rain-filled clouds

BACK TO THE FUTURE

The strong El Niños of recent years have caught the world's attention. But we are not the only generation to suffer the effects of this strange phenomenon — El Niños have been occurring for thousands of years. Scientists are even using history to help them track down future El Niños by looking at historical sources, including personal diaries, ships' logs, and rainfall records.

People who lived in Peru in past times, such as the Incas, were very aware of El Niño. In strong El Niño years, cities by the sea would be destroyed by terrible storms, and people were forced to move inland, into the mountains. Even here there was no escape, as El Niño years brought drought to these high regions. Historians are also finding links between El Niño and historical events all over the world, including revolutions and plagues. By looking at the past, perhaps we will find a way to predict future El Niños.

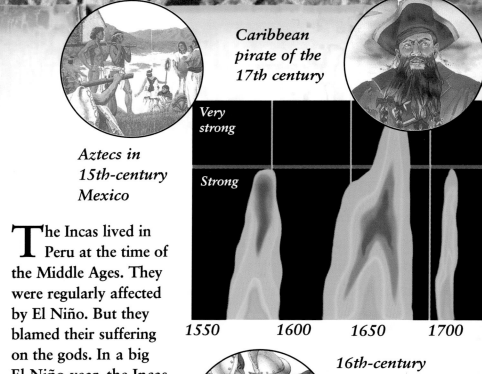

Caribbean pirate of the 17th century

Aztecs in 15th-century Mexico

Very strong			
Strong			
1550	1600	1650	1700

The Incas lived in Peru at the time of the Middle Ages. They were regularly affected by El Niño. But they blamed their suffering on the gods. In a big El Niño year, the Incas performed sacrifices to the gods (*below*). They hoped this would stop them from sending bad weather.

16th-century Spanish invaders

Throughout history, many different people have been affected by El Niño.

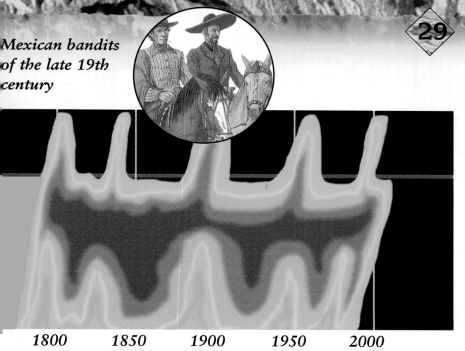

Mexican bandits
of the late 19th
century

1800   1850   1900   1950   2000

American
soldiers in
the mid-
19th
century

Aid
workers
in the
20th
century

UNCOVERING THE PAST

The first exact date we have for an El Niño is 1567. Before this, scientists do not know what people thought of the droughts or rains that sometimes wiped out their crops. Now scientists are beginning to piece together a record of El Niño years (*see chart, left*). One of the ways they have been able to do this is by reading the logbooks of 18th-century European sailors. These sailors noted odd events, including coastal waters that were turned strange colors by El Niño and seas that were suddenly home to animals such as alligators, sea snakes, and sharks.

ANCIENT EL NIÑOS

Scientists are now drilling deep holes into the Antarctic ice to find out about ancient weather. A new layer is added to the thick ice every year. Each layer shows changes in climate for that year, like the rings on a tree trunk. The scientists have found El Niño years going back at least 1,500 years. Some big events lasted for over 18 months.

El Niño may have stopped rain from falling in ancient Egypt. Farmers in Egypt (*below*) still depend on the Nile River's yearly floods to provide a layer of rich soil for their crops. When El Niño dries up the rain, the Nile floods do not come. This can ruin the year's harvest.

Glossary & *TIMELINE*

Algae
Algae are simple organisms that live in oceans, lakes, rivers, ponds, and damp soil. Some types of algae drift or swim; others cling to rocks. Large algae are called seaweeds.

Array
An array is a group of objects arranged in some kind of pattern. "The array" is also used by meteorologists to describe the TOGA/TAO system.

Atmosphere
The air that surrounds the earth.

Blizzard
A severe snowstorm, usually with very strong winds.

Climate
The average weather in a region, such as temperature, wind, and rainfall.

Drought
A long period without rain. This damages or destroys crops and kills animals that need good water supplies to survive.

El Niño
The Spanish term for "Baby Jesus" or "Christ Child." This refers to the warming of the eastern Pacific Ocean first noticed by Peruvian fishermen. The term is now also used by scientists to describe the effect this warming has on the world.

Evaporation
When a liquid turns into a gas. For example, when the ocean is heated by the rays of the sun, the top layer turns into a gas, called water vapor. This forms clouds that later return to the ground as rain or snow.

Famine
A shortage of food. This often happens during droughts, but can occur during heavy flooding.

Flash flood
Violent and sudden floods that do not last long. They are usually caused by very heavy rainfall in one area.

Global warming
A slow increase in temperatures across the world. This may be caused by more of the sun's heat being trapped in the atmosphere by gases such as CO_2 (carbon dioxide), methane, and water vapor.

1524
Did Pizarro attack the Incas in an El Niño year?

17th century
Hurricanes wreck many ships.

19th century
Monsoons in India affected by El Niño.

Hurricanes
Violent tropical storms that develop over warm seas where seawater is heated by the sun.

Jet streams
Long, narrow currents of high-speed winds that blow 25,000–40,000 feet above sea level.

La Niña
The opposite effect to El Niño, when the waters of the eastern Pacific become colder rather than warmer.

Magnetosphere
The region of space around a planet or star (like the sun)

Radiosonde
Miniature radio transmitter that is carried by weather balloons and aircraft to measure temperature, air pressure, and water vapor.

Satellites
Natural objects or vehicles built to orbit the earth or other planets and moons. They are kept in orbit by the force of the planet's gravity. Many are used to send television and radio signals around the world.

Solar wind
The constant release of energy from the surface of the sun.

1998 El Niño causes mudslides in California.

1990 Satellite launch speeds up TOGA system.

that is dominated by the magnetic field. This field traps particles that form a barrier against solar wind.

Tidal waves
A series of huge sea waves caused by shock waves from an earthquake or volcanic eruption. Correctly called tsunami as they have nothing to do with tides.

TOGA/TAO system
The Tropical Ocean Global Atmosphere/Tropical Atmosphere Ocean array. This system uses buoys and tide gauges to measure the seawater in the tropical areas of the Pacific Ocean.

1982 El Niño causes drought in southern Africa.

Meterologists
Scientists who study the weather.

Radiation
Radiation is the release of energy by an object. For example, a radiator radiates heat, while the sun also radiates X rays and gamma rays.

WOCE
The World Ocean Circulation Experiment. A global project to improve our knowledge of the ocean from top to bottom.

Hurricanes are called typhoons in the Pacific Ocean and tropical cyclones in the Indian Ocean.

Index